Contemporary Poets of Dorrance (573)

ONLY

COLD

COLD

FIRE

By **CONNY SCHAFLANDER**

Dorrance & Company
Philadelphia

To Nancy, with the
singing heart –
                    Affectionately,
                        Mary Kay

                            '63

Nancy –
    This was written in
your red bedroom
on Forest – I hope you
like it!
        Conny Schaflander
            Weisman

FOR MY MOTHER

whose constant faith and love

made it come true

CONTENTS

TO HEAR THE CROW

Here I am,
At the halfway of my life
I look back,
Then look again.
Time to ask the mighty potentate,
Is this all?
Is my turn lost forever
To hear the crow?
Must I weary, still half young,
To let release my half old soul,
Or dare I dream a dream again
And hope it's not too late to love?
I need a dream to ease my heart
Now that time has taken meaning,
For each day shortens
As it hurries by
And presses me to know,
Am I foolish to hold to hope
Should I just let go?
Was there ever any truth
In my youth's sweet promise,
To hear the crow?

7

THIS IS THE DAY THE BUTTERFLIES DIE

This is the day, I knew it at once
The moment I opened my eyes.
I can't bear today
It gets harder each year,
To stay, while the butterflies die.
Long before noon
They'll cover the beach
Like millions of delicate flowers
Then come the gulls,
With their horrible screech,
Swooping to pick and devour.
Why is it today?
How do they know?
What makes them choose the beach?
Why don't they die,
Hidden away,
Out of the seagull's reach?

I WOULD SIT IN THE WILLOW TREE

Not a word to ease my pain,
Not a hand to soothe my soul,
Only empty swirls that turn and tease me.
I would sit in the willow tree
To let tears fall,
With only the breezes to hear me cry
And calm my soul.
I would bathe in an icy tarn
To wash my heart,
With only the fishes to see me try
And quiet my hurt.
I would soar with the swallow
To leave despair,
And tell only the stars my love has become
An empty prayer.

I KNOW ONLY OF COLD, COLD FIRE

So black, so silent, are the hills of my home,
So still, so empty, its sky,
So hollow a waste, no creature will run
Nor bird attempt to fly.
So cold and barren this Mother Earth
That nothing can grow or flower,
So dark the endless, eerie nights
That animals hide and cower.

This is the land that gave me birth,
The land of my child root.
I came from the scar of this blackened earth
And was nursed by its bitter soot.
I grew without sun, like the skeleton stones
That lie in the dead river bed,
Then was whipped by a wind that eroded my soul
Until all of its spirit was bled.

I know no world but these stony dells,
I know only of cold, cold fire.
There's no memory's bell to waken my heart
Or ring up nostalgic desire.
So black, so silent were the hills of my youth,
So empty the echos above,
That now I belong to this hollow land
And it is the home I love.

ME AND DESDEMONA

I curse the fate
That gave me to the Moor.
What wretched luck
To pick this brooding mate.
He's mad, really mad,
Far a blacker Moor, inside,
Than this world could ever know.
He's so tormented
That life's become
One maddened, frenzied dream.
He cloaks me in a shroud
Of green suspicion
And seeks for festered motive
In my heart.
He finds excuse to spy
So he can trap me,
His only peace comes
When he's locked me up.
I beg an end.
Let him take his knife
And slice my heart;
I can't bear this withering death.
Kill me now, my Moor,
That you may know,
I was a true and faithful
Desdemona.

WOE IS ME

Woman, why do you not beget me sons?
Sons, sons, and more sons?
Aarons, Abels, Ezras,
Davids, Joshuas and Samuels?
Why, do you not flower
My precious drops
Into fruit without thorns?
Into beauty without weakness?
Into strength and sons?

Woman, woman,
You must beget.
I give to you all secrets
Hidden in me
From my father's fathers.
Only in you
Do I lock my treasures,
For the sons I want
And the sons I must have.

They, too, shall beget
And their son's sons
Shall beget.
From one to the next
Each drop the same;
Each drop my drop,
Yet changed.
Woman, in you lies life,
My life,
Release it and beget.

THE DIVORCE OF I YOU—YOU ME

Sad man, I know you well;
Long were we part of each other,
I you-you me.
But now it's bitter gall that rules
The place our tender passions held
And spiteful hunger that bites and gnaws
For sweetmeats flesh can never sate.
We rage, like children, in vengeful lust
To prick and probe and hurt again,
Till just this burn of pain is left,
To warm the hearts that love once filled.
I know not why it's so, sad man,
That pain does weld not sever,
Though we were torn apart by our war of hate
And long to be free altogether—
The I of you and the you of me
Will be part of each other, forever.

THE LAST AND FINAL WISH

Swoop down, great hawk,
And take me,
I know you are there.
Once I ran from you
Now
I turn in surrender,
Wanting only
A calm eternal night
Of dreamless slumber.

Come,
Last and final lover,
Let me rest on your breast.
Swoop down,
Quickly,
Softly,
And take me
With numbing bliss,
Sweet death.

I'LL STAND FREE

You, up there, whom I forsook,
Sharpen my mirror's biting tooth.
I'll rip this veil and turn away
From the acrid tastes of agony.
I'll stamp out all the pitying sighs,
I'll still sweet pain's seductive cries,
I'll ease the fear that chokes my breath,
I'll calm the doubt that eats my flesh.

You, up there, whom I forsook,
Help me search the face of truth.
I'm a creature of cawing lies,
I'm a creature I despise.
I'll burn this shroud that fools my heart;
I'll tear the cawing lies apart,
I'll purge the vanity from my soul
And hold to truth's hot, burning coal.

You, up there, whom I accept,
Know this mortal soul has wept.
Smile, but do not pity me,
I'll win my struggle and stand free.

THE TIDES AND COMPULSIONS OF DESIRE

Bubbling and black, like hot liquid night,
Runs this river, I know,
Rushing along with such boiling might
Stones melt to molten coal.
Roaring out its challenge,
Pulling with hypnotic eye,
Its appetite endless and savage,
Its calm—a deceptive lie.
River, I know you; you run in my veins,
I've drowned in the tides of your flight.
You've been the source, and the end, of all pain,
My despair and my ceaseless delight.

THANK GOD

Man boy,
Ghoul of fright,
Take warmth
From woman's flesh.

Man boy,
Crucified shrike,
Take courage
From woman's breast.

Man boy,
Blister of hope,
Enough,
Woman is dry.

Man boy,
Thank God,
At last
All seeds must die.

IF YOU PITY MAN

Cover me, black shawl of night,
Hide me from shivering galls of fright.
Soot all the faces ugly with pain,
Shroud all the hearts that love has slain.
Cover, cover, torn bone,
Eaten away and rotting alone
And cover the flesh of stinking strife
That's died in this foul vomit of life.
Stay forever, merciful friend,
To cover the corpses of all lost men,
To hush the cries of earthly hosts
Who must live on, though they're really ghosts.
Then stay and darken life's lewd hunger
Gnawing away on us innocent plunder.
Black shawl of night, sorrow's friend,
If you pity man—you will never end.

YOU LET ALL TRAINS GO THROUGH

Do you know you're a monster?
Why are you a monster?
Because you're indifferent, that's why.
Yes, and because you were indifferent to them,
You are cruel,
Even evil.
What did you do to stop it?
Stand there and pick your nose?
Pious hypocrites,
You flush conscience down the toilet, daily,
Then pray on Sundays, so you won't go to hell.
You'd better pray and be afraid of hell
For you deserve to burn forever.
Selfish stones,
Beg God to be merciful to you,
As you were merciful
When you let all trains go through,
When you let all ovens burn,
When you let all children die,
At Treblinka.

MINE IS THE BLOOD

I AM THE FRUIT, THE SEED, THE TREE,
I AM THE BLOSSOM, THE GLORY, THE HEART,
I AM THE THORN OF EVERY CENTURY,
I AM HISTORY'S UNWANTED MARK.
I AM THE FIGHTER, THE SETTLER, THE
    WANDERER,
I AM THE STUDENT, THE SEER, THE FOOL,
I AM THE BLOOD OF THE HOLY TORAH,
I AM THE MYSTERY THEY CALL A JEW.

WHO ELSE?

I live in the elephant zoo,
And of course, people call me bizarre!
I have my reasons, you know,
But no one asks what they are.

It began when my very keen ear
Picked up an unusual sound,
So tragically torn with tears
That I followed and here's what I found:

Every dawn all the elephants kneel,
Then, they just cry and cry,
With such anguish they almost congeal,
While wailing their hearts at the sky.

They rock and moan and sob
Worse than banshees making prayers,
It must break the heart of God
That they cry and no one cares.

There is something they desperately long for—
What it is I shall never know,
But such torment's too great to ignore,
They're the saddest of all suffering souls.

Yes, I live in the elephant zoo
And it's strange that I make it my home
But who else hears the elephants cry,
And will come, so they don't cry alone?

CUCKOO

Tick, tock, you clock,
Spin time.
Ring each hour,
End each love.
Cuckoo, tick tock,
Cuckoo, to you,
From this sad bird
Who cuckoos back at time!
You've hurried fast my joy
But let pain linger.
Your ticking drops
Dilute my wines of love.
Your spider feet
Cobweb all my beauty,
Yet you'll not grant me favor
To slow your tick.
You know it takes an eon
To spin a dream
But will you wait?
No.
You hurry tick, tick on,
You cuckoo clock,
Spinning time.

JUST LIKE FAUST

Moon, like an owl,
You sit there and stare
While we ants are eaten
By worms of despair.
So I make you a witness
As I solemnly swear,
"My soul to the devil
If he answers this prayer."

Yes, I'll give my soul
For one perfect day,
Whatever it costs
I vow I will pay.
Burn me to cinder,
Sentence me lost,
I want twenty four hours
Regardless of cost.

Hold back the night,
Stand still the sun,
Tie up the winds,
Freeze fish in their run.
Just twenty four hours,
One perfect day,
Then to hell with my soul
When the time comes to pay.

LIKE EVERY FOOL

How endless,
This blossom's agony
Of scarlet bursts,

How cruel,
This vine podding death
With fertile thirst.

How sad,
To cling in fear
Like every fool,

How hopeless,
To crave the manna
All cadavers do.

How dry,
How stale,
Is paradise lost,

How bitter, bittersweet,
This kiss of life,
At any cost.

Today My Father Died

My father
My only father
Is dead

I turn back to life
Without him
A frozen stone
Wishing
We could trade

I would take his place
In death
If he
Could take mine here

He gave his strength
To help me
Face
My barren days

Now
I am alone
And
Am
Afraid

ABOUT THE NEXT TIME AROUND

Who am I?
Where did this tiny
Pinprick of uniqueness,
That makes me me,
Come from?
Is that my soul?
This house I live in
When it withers and dies,
Will I float like a cloud
To another planet,
Another life?
Is there a choice
In time, place and form?
Next time around
Could I be
A turtle?
A bird?
A monkey?
If my me becomes human again
Who will I love?
The same people I love now,
Disguised,
Or different ones?
Will I know my children,
They me?

What if,
When the scales are balanced,
I only deserve to be
Some very small thing
Like
A raindrop?
A grain of sand?
A speck of dust?
Or what if
I don't deserve to be
Anything at all
But am granted one last wish,
To return to life
For a final moment.
What would I choose to be
For that final moment
Of return,
I don't know???
Wait—
Maybe I do.
If I had just one moment
To come back and spend
Then I would give someone
A moment's pleasure
And choose to be
A kiss.

27

NO SAD SONGS FOR ME

No sad songs for me,
Scatter my ashes and let me be free.
When my time comes to wither and die,
Let me blow with the breezes under the sky.
I'll make each day a balmed delight
Then waft through the nubian nights.
I'll kiss the petals of summer flowers
And blow their scent to lonely hours.

No sad songs for me,
Scatter my ashes into the sea.
I want to swim in the heart of a whale,
To be an algae on a dolphin's tail,
Or join the waves that hit the shore
And kiss the sand forevermore.
But I'll always be with the wind and the sea,
Sing no sad songs for me.

THE SURRENDER

A tear came down your cheek,
A drop of bitter pain
Made from the blood of hope,
For all your hope lay slain.
No sign gave signal to defeat,
You stood there stricken stone
Then came surrender,
Down your cheek,
In one small tear, alone.

TOO LATE

Grey Sparrow,
>You thought yourself a nightingale,
>Now how still and cold you lie.
>Who clipped your tail?
>Who pulled your wings?
>Who left you on my sill to die?

>Now I'm too late, to give my love,
>To warm and fill your sparrow heart,
>Yet, you gave pleasure to my eye
>When surging, with your special joy,
>You left this sill to soar and fly.

Grey Sparrow,
>You were, indeed, a nightingale,
>Now how still and cold you lie.
>Who clipped your tail?
>Who pulled your wings?
>Who left you on my sill to die?

"WE REGRET TO INFORM YOU"

From my little black pit
I mourn,
Scalded by grief
That does not spend.
I am held
In the stillness of my pain
And turned to frozen echo.

What to tell my heart?
That time will pass
And lock you to memory, forever?
What to do with this love,
But armor my heart
Then put it away
To remember.

31

THE BEGINNING—AND NOW

The beginning was long ago—
I, the child of loneliness,
Played in shadows
And heard the sounds of brook
And breeze
But not the sounds called love.

In my forest
I knew only the ferns and trees,
My images and dreams,
So I cared for them
And nothing else.
I did not have the gift called love.

That was the beginning—this is now.
Still I play in shadows and dream,
Still I love the image of those dreams
But I love all else too.
For time has taught me well, to know and give
The gift called love.

WOMAN'S CURIOUS POWER

I will wait
For you to know
You love me
For you must label
Every wave that tugs your heart,
Weigh and measure
All your grains of feeling;
Then stand apart
To add up all the best.

While I
Have no need
To give my heart this test,
For I possess
A woman's curious power.
All was settled
By my sure instinct,
One, two, three,
In our first magic hour.

TO A MOST DISTANT STAR

You've been long in the dark,
A lone and distant star,
Hidden from all suns.
Your fire's become a cold fire,
Your core an ancient rock.
You must turn to face this sun
And let your sad heart warm
To the healing of my love—
For love is the only light
That ends the dark forever.

NOTE TO A LOVER

All through the night
You warmed me with desire.
Your breath on my cheek,
Your whispers in my ear,
Melted me to love.
Now I lie alone,
Colder than cold,
Too empty without you.
Come back tonight,
Tender lover,
I need you.
The hours are wasted
Until we love.

AFTER

How warm are these moments after,
When our love's been fulfilled anew,
How happy is muffled laughter
And the completeness
That's only with you.

TAKE A TIGER

Golden lion, since we've loved,
I have need for only you.
When you leave for you own land
Take this stripéd tiger, too.

We must lose this dying jungle
And the bed of molten rock,
Not for us the monkey's struggle
Nor the vulture's screaming mock.

Now to roam the amber veldtland,
Eat the orchid, drink the dew.
Golden lion, take this tiger,
To warm the jessamine nights, for you.

A SHORT BLOOM

How soon are kisses cold,
Their flavor thin?
Almost before desire is bold
And love can begin.

How soon does sweet embrace
Yearn to pull apart?
Almost before the heated race
Has signaled its start.

How soon does passion's flower
Wilt for sleep?
Almost before love's ardor
Can sow and reap.

WHEN THE SAD WIND BLOWS

On this day
Our love did die,
But I'll not bury it
In the ground.
That's not the way to do it.
Instead a bonfire,
High as the sun,
Let the whole world see its light.
There I'll burn our love
To a fine bitter dust
And scatter the ashes free,
So you can never forget
When the sad wind blows
That it's ME,
             ME,
                   ME.

THANK YOU NOTE

Well, it's over,
Time to let you go
And stop this sighing,
I've no regrets.
I loved you,
More than any other woman
Ever could.
I understand you,
Better than any other woman
Ever will.
Would I have started
Knowing this sad end?
Yes,
For it's been good to love you
And I'm glad I did,
With no regrets.

A SWEET AND WILD HONEY

I keep the mirror of our love
Locked in darkened vaults,
I dare not look at its reflection.
Then would I yearn, in mighty waves,
To press against you once again
And taste the love we used to taste
That was sweet as wild honey.
For only in the allspice of our love,
Cleaving tight, in oneness, to each other,
Soldered ever closer by desire,
Have I ever known such a joy
Or tasted such a sweet and wild honey.

THE END OF A LONG GOODBYE

It's now goodbye,
To my true and constant love,
To my first and real love,
It's now goodbye.
I haven't come to you,
Yet from my night's dark tunnel,
How I've longed.
But I can never come to you again,
Now emptiness must fill my need,
That's all you left me.
Prophets say,
Time lessens pain,
Even makes it fade,
I wish it true,
For this pain I hold
Is much too big
To have to hold forever.
I know I've mourned
Our love's sad end
Far past all time of reason.
Now I lay my dead grief down
And ask, at last, release.
I can cling no longer
To the stillborn stone that's left.
This day marks the end
Of our thousand days
And the end
Of my long goodbye.

NOW THERE ARE ONLY THE FIREFLIES

Here in the dark I am empty,
Nothing can make me smile,
Only these fleeting fireflies
That glow every little while.
Waltz, fireflies, you are mine,
Tonight you belong to me.
Weave around my arbor,
Spin light in each bush and tree.

Light a forgotten happiness,
Spark memories of past desire,
Bring him to my heart once more
So I remember his warmth and fire.
It was such a sweet love
We shared and came to know,
Yet, now there are only you fireflies
And your temporary glow.

I ASKED THE SPHINX

What is love?

    It is warmth in a cold world,
    It is light in a dark world,
    It is joy in a sad world,
    It is over so soon.

Why is it over so soon?

    Because we don't love ourselves,
    Because we don't respect each other,
    Because we're misers in what we give,
    Because man is only human.

What makes man human?

    His great intellectuality,
    His great creativity,
    His great adaptability,
    His great need for love.

Why does man need love?

    Because it's a cold world,
    Because it's a dark world,
    Because it's a sad world,
    Because it's over too soon.

WIND, WIND

What a wind blows today,
It's blown my dreams worlds away.
It's caressed the peach trees glowing bright
And turned this day into cloved delight.

Wind, wind, catch my sorrow,
Give it to the geese to borrow,
Send them winging over the lea
To sing it out in honks of glee.

Wind, wind, take my heart,
Find its fated counterpart.
Search all the land and all the sea,
Bring back the one who matches me.

Hurry wind, how long you take
To find my true and destined mate.
Somewhere he yearns alone and blue
Not knowing I am yearning too.

IT'S MY TIME TO COCK-A-DOODLE-DOO

Who kissed these lips with April's breath
And woke my stony winter's heart;
Then stirred the thorns of sleepy flesh
That now the milkweed saps do start?
Oh Bonnie breath, oh Bonnie kiss,
What gentle dreams of spring I sigh,
Of greenest leaves, that shadow trysts,
Where love and chirpie birdies lie.
Awake, awake, dear hopeful fool,
And cock-a-doo your April's song.
Awake, awake, it's your time to cock-a-doodle-doo.

CHALLENGE

Listen fate,
I challenge you now.
Face to face,
I damn and dare you
To strike me a blow.
See can you break me?
You cannot!
For I have already bathed in tears
And stroked a dying heart—
I am not afraid.
What is there to lose
Music?
Love?
Dreams?
Well then,
Take them.
I hold a secret, hidden spark
That you can never touch,
Called will
And you cannot break my will.
Defiance was my mother,
Joy my father,
I was born a giant
And this life belongs to me
Not you.

I WHO AM PART

This world,
That is home to a swarming multitude,
That is cold, warm, sweet, bleak,
That is mountain, jungle, desert, stream,
This world,
No matter its face,
Is the world I love.

These multitudes,
Who surge with will to live,
Who are young, old, fighting, dying,
Who are black, white, green, yellow,
These multitudes,
No matter their color,
Are the multitudes I love.

This world,
These multitudes,
Are beautiful and reverent
And I who am part,
Of this world and these multitudes
Am reverent,
With love for them.